Copyright © 2021 Tekkan
Artwork Copyright © 2021

All rights reserved.
First Printing, 2021
ISBN 978-1-7363537-5-2

To contact Tekkan please email:
buddhaboy1289@gmail.com

How to Read My Poems

I want to be direct in my meaning — I want people to clearly understand my meaning. My wordiness is inspired by Shakespeare, and the (aimed-for) concision is in imitation of Japanese style. Using the sonnet with the tanka, I mix the sensibility of the Occident and the Orient — which I have done by living in England, Japan, and America.

I have married the sonnet to the tanka. Often, I don't rhyme my sonnets, because I want freer expression. I tell a story in the sonnet — using three quatrains separated by line spaces, and a final couplet. The story builds to a conclusion in the couplet. The tanka is a commentary, or a counterpoint, to the sonnet — the combined poems have two endings.

Recently I have added limericks, doggerel, and rhymed sonnets into my repertoire. The limericks have a rhyme scheme but the tanka do not.

I don't punctuate much in my poetry. I want the words themselves to do the work. There is logic between words, and the forms provide structure. By not using punctuation I hope to direct readers to carefully attend to each word — to appreciate the graininess of words.

Reading my poems silently and reading them
Aloud may be different experiences. When
I'm not rhyming my sonnets, there's not
always a pause intended at the end of the
line.

Hint: *unrhymed sonnets are to be recited not as lines but as phrases, and a phrase often overflows the break at the end of a line. I pause and take a breath where it seems natural for me to pause. Another person may pause differently than I do.*

Each poem is a piece of a mosaic, and it is
my hope that the collection of poems forms
an accurate portrait of consciousness.

My friend, *Will Ersland*, is a wonderful artist.
His artwork graces the cover of this book. My
daughter Jocelyn Suzuka Figueroa painted the
willow and the fish.

I am Barry MacDonald. I received the *dharma*
name *Tekkan*, which means "Iron Man," a
settled practitioner of great determination.

— *Tekkan*

Everyday Mind XXII

Cloudless morning sky
warms gradually —
some of the white roses
are already wilting.

My roses bloom when summer arrives
Sunny mornings in June are often cool
When the sun and the roses harmonize
That the roses don't last long is the rule
Year after year my rosebushes blossom
They are mostly white with a tinge of pink
That the sky is cloudless happens often
The mild weather and roses are in sync
I do forget the rose's sweet perfume
I have to be close and inhale deeply
The scent is a cynosure of the bloom
It's the rule that roses appear briefly
Each single blossom is ephemeral
The joy of beauty is perennial.

When clouds are absent
when mornings are often cool
the sky is filled with
immeasurable sunlight
that just happens to be blue.

A week before I didn't know my speed
I was just estimating my mileage
Without a grasp of my average speed
I couldn't make use of such knowledge
But as soon as I go fast I can tell
Whether I am doing the same — or better
Now I know what I'm doing very well
Thanks to my new bicycle computer
This little gadget on my handlebars
Is changing my ideas of biking
I know exactly how fast and how far
I'm going and whether I'm improving
But the wind is a pivotal player
An unpredictable force of nature.

Now I'm a greyhound
measuring the minutes and
the distance from
one landmark to the next
from one day to another.

Of all the things going on in a day
Some things are worthy of celebration
Even if I'm having an awful day
Some elements are worth recognition
I don't come to writing casually
I'd like to see what's going to effervesce
And to leverage curiosity
So perceptions and words may coalesce
I give myself to what I attend to
Writing focuses my sincerity
It adds significance to what I do
One of the benefits is clarity
I'd like to be as light as a feather
But tough enough for all kinds of weather.

Crossing boundaries
of what happens and how I
respond I would like
to dissolve who I think I
am and be spontaneous.

Imagine being a fish in summer
Acclimated to persisting current
Would you be sensitive to bright colors?
How often would you resist the current?
Would you be aware of what water is?
Or have an idea of the river?
Would the surface be a strange kind of fizz?
Would other fish be flashes of silver?
Would you know that the river is narrow?
What would you think of the river's surface?
Would you happily wiggle your torso?
Would you recognize your tail's service?
How much of a change would come in winter?
Would you ever have to deal with splinters?

Imagine the shock
of the sudden grasp of an
eagle's sharp talons —
the wrenching departure
from a comfy dimension.

Do you think the trees remember last year?
Does the sky have a hint of memory?
Somehow all of the elements cohere
Life is woven together cleverly
We're growing on a mysterious sphere
This moment goes on interminably
Some of my memories are very dear
But over time they become fantasy
What I'm remembering is a veneer
Memory continues tediously
My eyes and nose and tongue and skin and ears
Are open to life continuously
Experience sometimes becomes severe
I hope I can manage to be sincere.

Am I choosing to
recall as I do or is
remembering a
happening continuing
itself — independently?

When riding my bicycle I am free
I am not compelled to be productive
There are the birds and dragonflies to see
The bright panorama is seductive
The wind's a potent force of contention
The more that I push the more it resists
But even so I do find my traction
Finding a suitable pace — I persist
I don't have to go fast — but I like to
No one is compelling my exhaustion
I expend myself because I want to
With a healthy urge for satisfaction
There's a purity of strength in motion
That balances disturbing emotion.

I tend to measure
my speed against the other
riders that I come
across in a curious
urge of compulsivity.

I don't want the need to feel important
Because then I am measuring myself
And I am seeking others' endorsements
And will be busy promoting myself
Also I have a yearning to be loved
To be comprehensively understood
To comport with someone like hand in glove
Savoring companionship would be good
I am wondering from where does love come?
I think love already resides in me
But my capacity is kind of numb
With too much disturbance to set it free
Love is always there waiting for income
I have to be ready to let it outcome.

Perhaps love is
a dexterous hand
ready to engage with
the earth and people
and I am the glove.

Books can be stuck describing what happened
It need not be necessarily so
I imagine a book without an end
That captures the present and helps it grow
Because miracles are happening now
The seasons repeat again and again
Life gets increasingly burdened somehow
Surprising disappointments are a drain
But there's no ending to this moment now
I can't comprehend all that's happening
It's all simultaneous anyhow
I'm trying to get good at balancing
Can I affix words to liberation?
Don't know — but it is my aspiration.

This moment goes
on and on and all
that goes along with it
is incomprehensible
until now.

Morning is drenched in the summer sunlight
Only a few clouds are drifting southward
The whole expansive river is alight
I'm trying to capture its life with words
The heat of the sun envelops my skin
A million leaves are reflecting the light
And the clouds and the river are akin
Gentle motion is concealing their might
How can one capture this moment now?
It is the point of creativity
Numberless species are living somehow
Emerging beings in activity
There's too much going on to pigeonhole
My viewpoint is only a buttonhole.

In this happenstance
moment the river and the
wisps of the clouds are
progressing gradually
majestically southward.

I'm not going to think about her — not now
Yes — she is beautifully intelligent
I can't get ahold of her anyhow
And I'm wary of her temperament
I'm not naïve with people anymore
The way she hooked me was remarkable
With no explanation she closed the door
And she has made herself unreachable
It's not good to dwell on her lovely eyes
So piercingly intent and powder blue
I really don't think that she told me lies
After all there is nothing I can do
If I let myself go — then I'm to blame
I'm not going to be a moth drawn to flame.

Certainly she has
a most bodacious body
with such fetching curves
but I'm beyond those baubles
with important things to do.

A girlfriend would be inconvenient
I would have to live so differently
Of course there would be our disagreements
When I'd rather act independently
We would be spending evenings on the phone
Going over what happened every day
I'd have to develop a firm backbone
To get at least a portion of my way
And I would have to rearrange my house
She would be over here some of the time
It would almost be like having a spouse
Which would be bodacious part of the time
If only desire could be controlled
But it can't — it just multiplies eightfold.

I'm safely ensconced
in my abode with only
the solicitous
attention of my rowdy
male cat for entertainment.

Sometimes I wake before I intend to
And I'm lying in bed ruminating
I'd like to sleep but I'm unable to
While my head is busy cogitating
Then I'm vulnerable and defenseless
I don't have thinking — the thinking has me
I'm exhausted but my mind is restless
I'm not present — I'm stuck in memory
My life appears as a hall of mirrors
Each reflection is grossly distorted
I am masculine and I don't shed tears
I keep my emotions closely guarded
Relaxation is a wonderful gift
Learning to relax is a handy trick.

I can adopt the
lotus posture before dawn
straightening my back
folding legs over under
breathing and quieting.

It's been so dry that the grass quit growing
With only occasional scraps of clouds
Mostly from the south the wind's been blowing
And blowing on the hills the wind is loud
I wouldn't notice if I weren't riding
The pressure of wind is manageable
Maneuvering in wind is like dancing
Finding the perfect pace is possible
There's joy in motion on my bicycle
There's nothing between me and everything
Perceptions are vibrantly physical
Rushing inside the wind is exciting
I push myself approaching exhaustion
I relax achieving satisfaction.

When the wind pushes
me from behind the air is
quiet and I move
precipitously until
I turn and face its roaring.

The lift part of the bridge is in motion
And pedestrians wait at a closed gate
We riders too wait in position
The gate releases — I become the bait
Going first I leave him following me
Gliding smoothly through the crowd of people
Starting in the right climbing gear is key
I rise and dance lightly on my pedals
I've raced up this hill many times before
But usually I ascend alone
Climbing this hill is what I'm training for
I've made the slope a competitive zone
Near the top I shift to a faster gear
I don't suppose he is anywhere near.

Turning a corner
I glance behind to check for
him seeing him a
little ways behind as I
shift again increasing speed.

You surprised me again by coming here
Walking into my office with coffee
I've not thought about you — you disappeared
I did not forget about your body
You didn't bring the cups — you brought the pot
You are not a person to go halfway
When you do drink coffee you drink a lot
Doing a kind of coffee pot sashay
You're typically brash unconsciously cute
It appears that you've just got out of bed
Your breasts are looking like bulging grapefruits
For me not to see I'd have to be dead
It takes me a while to know what to say
This doesn't happen every other day.

I'm discombobulated
And inarticulated
My tongue is too slow
So my words don't flow
But I'm also elated.

You have certainly come animated
All you can do is to talk about Bruce
Just what I would have anticipated
Your soon-to-be ex is a complete louse
I say it's not worth getting agitated
And I'd like to talk about anything else
Now the way forward is indicated
He can sell the damn boat and keep the house
The divorce decree will be stipulated
You won't have to live with a drunken spouse
Aren't you happy to be liberated?
You're lucky to have gotten a townhouse
At least now I know where you're located
I don't understand why you're frustrated.

Put up with the frustration
Just do the mediation
Let the lawyers work
Don't go so berserk
You'll get your compensation.

I don't mind you coming into my life
Bursting suddenly into my office
I am not beholden to my ex-wife
And I don't want to appear standoffish
But I have questions — what happened to you?
And why did you stop returning my calls?
I wanted to talk but what could I do?
It was like you erected a brick wall
I don't know about your soon-to-be ex
From what you say he's not a nice person
It seems he has a scornful intellect
Your relationship now is going to worsen
I must say that I don't care about him
And the chances of Bruce changing are slim.

So what if he wants the boat?
Who cares if it even floats?
He may be swimming
With other women
But who cares if he's a goat?

It's just that I've been conflicted — she says —
My mind's been racing and I've been upset
And I get entangled in what he does
I have been lost in a crabby mindset
And I am not even charging my phone
I'm sorry that I've caused you to worry
But I'm spending most of my time alone
Please — could you find a way to forgive me?
I've missed your company and your kind words
Of all my friends — you — best — understand me
I've been so angry and also quite bored
I believe that you know how to help me
So — Barry — I don't know what I would do
Without a compassionate man like you.

I've had to move all my stuff
And every day has been rough
I have been weary
And also teary
I've already had enough.

She's given me a lot to think about
Can she truly not be charging her phone?
Divorce does make sensitive people pout
And I'm relieved that she says she's alone
Of all her friends I best understand her
And she chose to burst in on me today
I know the trials of divorce are severe
Few of us can really expect fair play
I don't like being left in the dark
I'm happy to be in contact again
We didn't say any unkind remarks
And perhaps both of us are under strain
I do suspect she knows what she's doing
I will not put up with any lying.

Before I had no answers
And couldn't make advances
I was damn lonely
My days were stony
I didn't like my chances.

This obsession over this girl is like
A fizzle in my consciousness skewing
My perspective and limiting what I
Could be experiencing even though

I'm not a novice in love and am well
Apprised of how such intoxication
Dissipates revealing imbalances
And disharmonies perhaps fixable

With sincere efforts towards empathy but
Probably not as I can attest with
Years of disappointment and so I ask
What am I doing indulging such an

Infatuation thereby foregoing
Uncluttered unburdened liberation?

With the mission of
obtaining kitty litter
and mouthwash walking
in Walmart's parking lot I
see the swallows have returned.

When asked how liberation appears a
Zen master said it's like everyday life
Except one is floating two inches off
Of the ground as I remembered in the

Parking lot of Walmart seeing a flight
Of swallows acrobatically swooping
And darting about the entrance dancing
In air having returned for the summer

From their migration south for a reason
That is known only to them they frolic
Around a strip mall in Minnesota
Showing that mundane human existence

Isn't separated from the vast and
Interwoven workings of the cosmos.

The swallows may be
looking down upon Walmart
on occasion but
not in condescension as
they are not at all snobs.

It's obvious what romantic love is
When I am dressed up in my clip-on shoes
And sleek fabric jersey slicing through the
Wind on my bicycle pedaling with

A practiced cadence through the countryside
For an hour into my ride when I come
To the cynosure and the ultimate
Test of my ride ascending the steep slope

To Holton when I rise from my seat and
Dance on the pedals and at apparent
Ease at first but somewhere along the way
I begin to strain and to gasp for breath

With every kick of the pedals as my
Entire consciousness narrows to a point.

The focused effort
of consciousness narrows
with the strain of a
lusting eliminating
the splendiferous cosmos.

I'm seeing monarch butterflies thinking
Maybe these are those that migrated from
Mexico or perhaps they are the next
Generation and I see them on the

Bike beating the air fluttering as they
Do in their peculiar fashion as I'm
Pumping my legs on a slope straining with
Effort in my breathing lungs and beating

Heart and yet my sight is stable and not
Like the butterflies that must be viewing
The world in a jerky sequence of ups
And downs and I'm guessing that they are not

Queasy with air sickness nor do they have
Vertigo as I suspect that I would.

The monarchs and I
are rotating with the earth
orbiting the sun
orbiting the Milky Way
expanding from the Big Bang.

I wasted my time in conversation
Yesterday aware of passing minutes
Considering how long I would stay with
Friends I haven't been able to meet with

For a year face to face because of the
Pandemic thinking soon I would go to
Do writing until I realized how
Stupid I was not to appreciate

Genuine friendship reunited in
The happy exchange of shared views making
The difference between the endurance
Of or the curious exploration

Of life wherein allies pique my thoughts and
Embolden me within difficult days.

Yesterday I did
not get to my writing
but instead the weight
of isolation lifted
in connection with friends.

In my daily passage of it on my
Bicycle I imagine the scope of
A field of soybeans of advances
Of knowledge over millennia and

Of the application of satellite
Analysis of the soil and of the net
Of regulations ruling each of the
Taxable acres and of the rise of

Corporate farms replacing family
Farms with the management of sowing and
Harvesting feeding international
Markets and affecting diplomatic

Relationships and worldwide appetites
Harnessing the sun the soil and water.

The surface of the
earth is continuing to
undulate over
millennia rising up
with mountains and eroding.

I assume Kitcat is chasing a bug
Bunching up the rug by the door but he's
Blocking something with his paws again and
Again and he's pouching and springing and

His tail is whipping and balancing his
Body and then I see the pitiful
Little black mouse frantically turning with
Kitcat inescapably hovering

Over him as they go thudding down the
Stairs to the basement as I go about
The business of changing the water in
His water dishes and refilling the

Container with cat food while listening
To commotion until quiet returns.

I rescue the third
dazed mouse with an injured
leg picking it up
with a towel and putting it
on the patio outside.

I think that I know what I'm doing but
Life has a way of revealing many
Delusions as I returned after a
Two-year absence to the dentist's office

For the scraping away of plaque and a
Polishing and for two types of X-rays
Involving unforeseen gadgets with the
Usual discomfort along with the

Attention of a female hygienist which
I like but this time she pronounced the term
"General recession" which the dentist
Explains means that my gums are receding

From my teeth and exposing some of the roots
And "no" the gums will not grow back again.

Three times a day when
using my electric tooth
brush it appears that
I've been applying too much
pressure which I now regret.

It's easy to be hypnotized by the
Edges of things into emphasizing
My separation within my skin from
The carnival of events happening

Continually around me such as
With the lacerating suddenness of
A bald eagle flying and clutching a
Fish in its talons or with the motion

Of a willow tree on a summer day
While I am trying to realize that
Wherever I am looking there isn't
A separation between events but

Only a flowing of happenings in
All directions like ripples of water.

I can't help making
distinctive demarcations
between happenings
one after another but
choosing is arbitrary.

My daughter Jocelyn is using the
White of primer to paint on white fabric
Reviving photographic images
Snapped by her Japanese great-grandfather

When he was an Imperial soldier
In on the conquest of China eighty
Years ago capturing the instant when
A young troop while standing was reading the

Similar ink writings between China
And Japan on a magazine cover
And if I look at the painting today
From one angle the image is gray but

If I look from the opposite view it's
A distinctly white and ghostly image.

Do you suppose in
the instant of the photo
the soldier could have
imagined eighty years on
This result of the photo?

Brushing before dawn used to be the high
Point of the day for us when I would turn
Him on his back and brush from beneath his
Chin to tail and then I'd brush his back and face

After which we'd have a contest of wills
And dexterity when he'd flip himself
To his back and I'd slap him with both my
Hands all over him as he tried to bite

My fingers which he sometimes did and he
Would often yowl during the contest but
One day he decided not to play the
Game anymore and immediately

After the brushing he left me sitting
Uselessly on the floor watching him leaving.

It dawned on me that
my elusive slapping may
have caused frustration
to accumulate until
Kitcat decided to quit.

I would like to celebrate the humble
Cucumber that I buy in the produce
Part of the grocery store to adorn
My toasted ham and cheese sandwich every

Lunch because although its taste is quite bland
It provides my consciousness with the salve
That I am eating my vegetables
And it's amazing the number of days

Through which I can consume but a single
Cucumber by slicing judicially
Thinly and even the procedure of
Cutting a cucumber brings me a tinge

Of satisfaction as it's civilized
Easy and not unpleasant to gaze on.

I am biased to
believe a cucumber
is not a fruit but
a vegetable because
I do need to eat veggies.

o to be archy the poet who died
and was born again in the body of
a cockroach laboring ceaselessly to
express himself by jumping off of the

frame of a typewriter headfirst to strike
a key to make a letter composing
in a day of hard labor a simple
short poem without the benefit of

capital letters because he couldn't
work the shift key and yet during the night
freddy the rat another poet would
come and eat the paper destroying the

earthly record of archy's prodigious
efforts reducing life to misery.

don marquis the
journalist created the
idea of the
unfortunate poet in
imitation of himself.

Cobwebs in the corner of the windows
And motes of dust floating in the air and
A wasp bobbing and momentarily
Resting on a leafy hedge outside of

The window amid the intense light of
The summer sun ascending to a good
Height in the morning perhaps leads one to
believe nothing much is going on but

No as the heat is warming my skin to
The verge of sweat and I look under
The brim of a straw hat with a weave of
Gaps through which the sun sparkles but also

Somewhat shields my eyes from the glare I am
Liberated enough to be relaxed.

One doesn't need a
reason for relaxing but
being able to
in vexing circumstances
is a propitious ploy.

Sometimes I'd rather not compose poems
Of significance as I would have to
Summon a serious attitude which
I have to do often enough so now

I will recount the saga of buttering
Two slices of toast improving them with
A layering of ham and cheese to be
Superimposed with cucumber which I

Slice with loving care after which I make
My way to the couch to settle myself
Upon to watch the *Tour de France* while I
Inattentively move to take a bite

But then my fingers fumble and a slice
Of the cucumber drops and vanishes.

I couldn't find it
anywhere until I saw
the dust-bespotted
slice of cucumber had rolled
a good way across the room.

I do like to talk to you everyday
And it's easy to be in touch by phone
It's important for me to have my say
As I think about you when I'm alone
As soon as I'm awake I love to call
And now you're answering every morning
It was hard for me when you put up your wall
But now I'm excited that we're talking
At 5 a.m. I'm calling your number
While lying in bed I'm talking to you
Our conversation allays my hunger
I yearn to talk and it seems you do too
Every morning we're having pillow talk
Sometimes I wake early and watch the clock.

Your idea to
talk on the phone at 5
a.m. before dawn
is a wonderful way to
start my day — thinking of you.

So with new habits I have to adapt
I am delaying my meditation
And rejiggering my schedule in fact
Causing more than a little disruption
I love to be able to interact
Stimulated by our conversation
Your voice is having a touching impact
Feeding an urge for anticipation
I am soaking up your daily doings
Getting to know your intimate habits
Becoming familiar with your thinking
Appreciating your verbal talents
And after our predawn conversation
I am digesting new information.

Pillow talk
predawn intimacy
is becoming the
cynosure
of my days.

You don't trust Bruce and he owes you money
You still share an account at Bremer Bank
There's a circumstance that's kind of funny
An opportunity to play a prank
He has been on a list for twenty years
To be a member of the country club
Now his number is up — his way is clear
He has $4,000 to pay up
He thinks that he can be a golfing fool
All he has to do is to pay the fee
He's clearly forgotten you know the rules
And you intend to withdraw that money
When he writes a check he will be surprised
His cherished wish will have to be revised.

The mediators
haven't decided on the
dispursal of funds
so he's not entitled to
claim his golfing membership.

Your Daddy was a smart entrepreneur
And he once owned a lumber company
And he was a successful inventor
With a patent earning lots of money
He wasn't a very faithful husband
And put your mother through enormous grief
He's reminding me of your ex-husband
There's a pattern here — that is my belief
Your Daddy drank a lot of alcohol
Normal behavior in your family
He would go to bars and get into brawls
And he died before the age of fifty
Your family did enjoy prosperity
Then suddenly you lived in poverty.

It's astounding how
drinking's a thread woven
through generations
of your family — also
affecting your brother's life.

You remember a good friend from childhood
You were swimming together at the beach
She wore a tight bathing suit with a hood
The fabric was so very tightly stretched
She was protruding and looking silly
And you couldn't stop yourself from laughing
She had chubby cheeks and a big belly
It was obvious you hurt her feelings
And you do remember feeling guilty
But the damage had already been done
You wavered between laughter and pity
While your outburst kind of ruined the fun
There's so much trauma — even from grade school
Kids can be unintentionally cruel.

You told your Dad the
story afterward because
you did feel guilty
but in the telling the two
of you couldn't stop laughing.

Your family was happy for a while
Until about your junior high school age
Your Dad dying suddenly was a trial
Your Mom struggled to make a living wage
She was forced to work a couple of jobs
There was persisting insecurity
But she did persevere against the odds
Hardship brought you early maturity
Difficulty marred your adolescence
The loss of your Daddy was a burden
He was such a dominating person
You missed his calming masculine presence
Losing your Dad was a calamity
But your Mom came through for the family.

Your Dad was a rogue
dynamically exciting
and afterward the
quiet absence in the house
was difficult to endure.

In high school you were a popular girl
You dated the football quarterback star
Those years went by in an ecstatic whirl
And I believe they made you who you are
Truthfully you didn't care about him
Your personalities didn't quite fit
He was more often suited to the gym
After graduation you knew you'd split
But you liked getting so much attention
You were talkative — you were sociable
Faux celebrity was your dimension
All this information is notable
I understand your personality
How you formulate rationality.

To me you appear
as a queen of beauty a
little worse for wear
with the slightest tinge of
dissipation about you.

After high school you attended college
At the university in Duluth
You enjoyed learning and gaining knowledge
You met Bruce and comprehended the truth
You understood his cast of character
He was a rogue and a heavy drinker
You guessed that he'd be a good provider
With him you found genuine desire
With him you had what we call chemistry
Your personalities bonded with glue
And should we say that's serendipity?
In the end it didn't work out for you
He makes a sport of disparaging you
He isn't nice — as you already knew.

Sometimes it's a shame
that like attracts like and with
time the qualities
bringing couples together
may end up destroying them.

You left college without graduating
You married and he finished his degree
His job is financially rewarding
And you started having a family
He does electrical engineering
He returned to get a master's degree
Enabling him to begin managing
Which earns an even higher salary
For him you gave up your education
Which now has become a major regret
Being limited is a frustration
Being unsupported is quite a threat
You take so much pride in both of your sons
Raising them is the best thing you've done.

You are counting on
a substantial amount of
spousal support from
the divorce decree which is
entirely justified.

You went to work when your kids entered school
And you really do enjoy waitressing
His disapproval is certainly cruel
Your freedom is beyond his controlling
You have always loved being sociable
And you are being paid to talk all day
Conversing is more than comfortable
Bantering with customers is child's play
You're getting the attention you desire
You have many relationships at work
You've transformed yourself into a server
Having wide social contact is a perk
It irks him that you are cute and friendly
That so many are complimentary.

There is a guy who
every year is buying you
a Christmas tree as
a kind of a fetish which does
tend to make Bruce unhappy.

I have never known such intimacy
My ex and I weren't nearly as fluent
I'm learning details with intricacy
I do not believe this is imprudent
Who would have believed that at 5 a.m.
I'd be talking to a lovely woman?
I'm surprised at how elated I am
I think I'm becoming fully human
New experience is blooming for me
Digesting the world through another's eyes
Conversation is good — and we agree
And communication is best without lies
Every day when I'm getting out of bed
Thoughts of her are occupying my head.

For the rest of the
day I'll be considering
new information
and how differently life
appears from another view.

I had a friend in Hutchinson Kansas
It was my first taste of companionship
With him I knew an easy happiness
I remember our genuine friendship
And fifty years on I don't recall much
But I'm aware of a hole in my heart
So much of my life I've felt out of touch
I am familiar with living apart
It's not been easy to communicate
I've put it down to mismatched chemistry
With people I tend to reach a stalemate
I live with a dose of perplexity
For easy companionship it's a must
For intimacy I have to have trust.

My family moved
from Hutchinson Kansas
to Minnesota
where in Bayport the kids
were nasty and combative.

Playing with words comes easily to me
I like to express what I'm perceiving
When saying what I want I do feel free
Clarifying my thoughts is exciting
With most people there is hesitancy
There are hidden barriers in the way
I've come to keep my distance guardedly
And too often I don't know what to say
Pristine sheets of paper open to me
I can express exactly what I want
The receptive paper and I agree
I've found a reliable confidant
There is a purity in playing with words
And I don't care if I'm sounding absurd.

The presence of the
paper serves as the best of
friends until it may
happen that a flesh and blood
person comes along I hope.

For some reason we can articulate
Conversation comes without an effort
She bandies her phrases and innovates
Our manner of relating does comport
She tells her story and it resonates
She's in a distressing situation
And for her — isolation suffocates
It's better to express the frustration
Perhaps some solutions may percolate
I'm not going to tell her what she should do
While talking — ideas may germinate
And she may grasp what she already knew
Listening carefully can be a game
I really do believe she feels the same.

If she hadn't called
me there was no way that I
would have taken the
initiative to call her —
she is uninhibited.

She understands how attractive she is
I'm astounded that she's talking to me
I know how intoxicating she is
And comprehend that there's no guarantee
I'm weighing implications in her words
Speculating what she feels about me
Nothing she is saying goes unexplored
I feel the sting of insecurity
I want to be cared about — to be loved
With her is that a possibility?
Presently the question is unresolved
The truth will emerge eventually
She is bursting with sexuality
Topping pleasing compatibility.

I don't like being
exposed but I'm already
hooked and excited
so I'm going to keep talking
and see what eventuates.

Suppose you imagine how life could be
Without the burden of inhibitions
From my point of view you're already free
You are able to change your conditions
Which you are doing by talking to me
Not being bound by self-definitions
But don't always expect to be carefree
Don't waste energy in competition
Problems with solutions tend to agree
You're not liking your present position
So envision where you would like to be
Which could be an open proposition
Perhaps judgment day for a divorcee
May well turn out to be a jubilee.

Why drag around
all those old arguments and
bitter memories
when you could be learning the
best lesson — how to relax?

Most of my anguish comes from my thinking
I don't notice what it's doing to me
I'm not supple — I'm only reacting
I would like to use spontaneity
It's a matter of developing poise
Relaxing is a propitious game
Reducing my troubles to background noise
I don't have to struggle argue and blame
So how may I relax when I want to?
Relaxing is a trick that takes practice
Of releasing thinking when I need to
My thoughts are like a prickly cactus
I accept that I may not get my way
I'll do something else on another day.

I rely on a
simple idea of a
power greater than
myself that I partner with —
this power takes care of me.

Relaxing is the hardest trick there is
Because I don't think about doing it
I concentrate on doing my business
Without a success I don't want to quit
But my relationships don't work like that
Especially when involving affections
I'm not good at manipulating that
Compelling people in my direction
I cannot make people care about me
Perhaps lovers grow into each other
I have to relax and to let things be
Somehow companions find one another
Being cheerful is very attractive
It has to be true to be effective.

I practice being
lonely and cheerful at the
same time trusting
wonderful developments
are just around the corner.

Something about me tickles your fancy
We've been conversing now every morning
I'm liking our talk — it makes me happy
Starting the day with you is exciting
We're saying hello right at 5 a.m.
There are always new topics to explore
I don't want to be hungry — but I am
I'm surprised that you're eager — but you are
The hours we're talking are filling my day
They make me ponder for deeper meanings
Afterward I consider what you say
I'm looking to foster new beginnings
Conversing on the phone every morning
Every evening is worth the waiting.

To hear your voice say
my name at 5 a.m. when
most people are still
sleeping has a certain thrill
worth the anticipation.

All relationships are perishable
I think this is something you understand
Not only if you're incompatible
Even with your sincerity on hand
Over time people grow differently
And they come to grate against each other
We all have quirks of personality
So it's good to forgive one another
But relationships don't have to perish
Can you give your partner a gentle touch?
And refrain from imposing your answers?
But who am I to talk so overmuch?
These are questions that I haven't mastered
There is something that's beyond chemistry
A loving patience is a remedy.

Maybe I'm a great
fool to be talking like this
as I'm divorced too
and spending my holidays
as a singularity.

You're angry at the cook for what he said
He accused you of being "such a woman"
It certainly seems that he's a blockhead
You could have said he's a troglodyte man
There's a lot going on at your café
Your friend Sherry is a likeable girl
She can make a new boyfriend every day
From your description she's like a showgirl
No wonder Bruce got so jealous of you
You're enjoying a vibrant social life
And I really have to give you your due
You're more than an ordinary housewife
I do like using the word "cynosure"
I think you possess plenty of allure.

Meanwhile I am all
by my lonely self at the
office going through
essays correcting grammar
redoing faulty syntax.

How lucky we were to find each other
It's so simple to have conversation
To listen and talk to one another
While cultivating our relaxation
I'm curious how your days are going
I'm giving you my eager attention
The littlest details are engaging
Enlivening our daily narration
And I also get to talk about me
And to express all of my hidden thoughts
You're giving me the opportunity
I'm getting to untie my secret knots
You're helping me discover who I am
To say what I think — and not give a damn.

It's only because
you are listening to me
that I have the chance
to express my daily thoughts
that would have been forgotten.

You're saying that Sherry is a real tease
She doesn't care about the men she knows
She doesn't go out of her way to please
Her availability is a pose
These poor guys will do anything for her
Lacking a clue of her indifference
She's turning love into a ligature
Their sincerity makes no difference
You don't appreciate her behavior
You're saying it reflects her bitterness
She's getting back at the guys who've hurt her
She's completely consumed with unhappiness
She's already divorced — three times over
Nothing's worse than a disgruntled lover.

Taking orders at
the café is the perfect
ploy for snaring the
unsuspecting fools who
eagerly keep showing up.

I feel some pressure to make things happen
I'm infatuated with this woman
Emotions kickstart my adrenaline
I want to be her only leading man
But she is talking to plenty of guys
While I'm stuck in my office by myself
With Bruce I'm beginning to empathize
Like him I feel deserted on a shelf
I'm building up the nerve to ask her out
I feel impelled to seize the momentum
I can't be inhibited by my doubts
I've got uncertainty to overcome
I just can't be quiet — I have to move
I've got my masculinity to prove.

The aching yearning
of love forced me to ask her
out on Friday night
and we'll be meeting at a
fancy Chinese restaurant.

I am beginning to feel the weight of
A sickening familiarity
She said yes — giving me more to dream of
This doesn't solve my insecurity
I'm anticipating our coming date
And imagining how she'll dress for me
Excited daydreaming is really great
It has the appearance of being carefree
But now my emotions are invested
I'm starting to yearn for certain results
Because I know nothing is guaranteed
Moderating myself is difficult
I want to see that she cares about me
This harrowing feeling won't let me be.

I'd like to wrench out
my insecurity and
be as casual
and as nonchalant as a
forgetful Lothario.

She does enjoy my sensitivity
Savoring my able conversation
She likes my easy creativity
I think I'm winning her admiration
She says she wants to keep talking to me
It helps to lessen her aggravations
She's feeling a taste of despondency
And experiencing wild gyrations
She's getting divorced and can't let it be
Her future income is a fixation
She does need money to live happily
Her love is worth some remuneration
She's not letting Bruce get off easily
She demands to be treated decently.

I do wish that she
would forget about Bruce as
obviously he's
a bully and a drunk and
how can that be attractive?

There's a paradox in liberation
At least of the type that I am seeking
Trying too hard creates separation
I'd like to give up the habit of grasping
There is the initial desperation
A lingering period of suffering
That's enough to inspire frustration
That culminates in a new beginning
From there what's needed is relaxation
A peace apart from unending striving
Fascination with subtle vibrations
There is patience to be cultivating
I want to surf with my motivations
I would like to balance with emanations.

Romantic love and
political victory
may be delusions
to be grasped only for a
moment before they dissolve.

Our evening together went splendidly
And it ended with a lingering kiss
Leaving me dreaming again hungrily
Thinking of ways that we could coalesce
She wants to keep on talking frequently
And again tomorrow in the morning
Which I'm looking forward to eagerly
To begin the day with our conversing
But something seems a little odd to me
I think I'm noting a little distance
She's parceling affections carefully
I'm getting a sense of some resistance
She is not as open as she could be
So I will play along and wait and see.

Our rendezvous on
the phone as I'm lying
in my bed and she's
sitting up drinking coffee
isn't quite enough for me.

Do people fall in love — and recover?
I wonder why we use the word "falling"
Like jumping out of a plane together
To experience a weightless floating?
This changes my sense of reality
Fixing my attention on a lover
Perhaps it's happening naturally
Involving obstacles to get over
Passion is taking so much attention
I don't want to live like this everyday
It is a constant and stressful tension
Straining to find exciting things to say
And my lingering doubts won't let me be
That perhaps she is only teasing me.

The necessary
details of getting through the
ordinary chores
of my daily life do make
me increasingly weary.

She says on the phone that she enjoys me
She suspects I don't know my influence
That I have an intriguing history
And sometimes my words cast a kind of trance
That I'm not like the other guys she's known
There's depth and breadth that is exceptional
And that when her thoughts won't let her alone
I'm helping her to be more flexible
It's true — each situation is unique
And can be viewed from different angles
There are various solutions to seek
When stubborn attitudes are untangled
But most of all she likes my gentle touch
And she likes my attention very much.

She doesn't know the
influence she's having on
me as I struggle
with my equanimity
and with love's uncertainty.

I choose cyclical over linear
Time putting faith in the rising and the
Setting of the sun and the orbiting
Of the earth around the sun producing

The seasons demonstrating the constant
Arising and disintegration of
Things even as I experience age
And so many of the people I've known

Live only now as a diminishing
Memory surely to vanish with me
But the fact of consciousness is so odd
Why shouldn't we suppose it continues

And rejoice because we don't have to earn
The perpetual beating of our hearts?

Perhaps like winter
death is only a season
of life which bursts its
bonds and blooms again into
youth and curiosity.

The idea that birth and death happen
Only once makes the pivotal moments
Of adolescence and young adulthood
And middle age so much more fretful as

Opportunity must be seized or lost
Forever and then how much weightier
Does remorse become with consequences
And how much sharper are resentments toward

People who get in the way and how much
More fearful does the future appear as
An end is coming as a monstrous void
Liable to create terrors of mind as

Of being buried alive unable
To breathe in suffocating loneliness.

We are just conscious
enough to be forced into
making conceptions
about the passage of time
and about our own demise.

My quiet attention allowed me to
See without the hinderance of stray and
Meaningless repetitive thoughts a crow
Land on the grass and utter its caw in

A guttural manner with its throat and
With its beak and then I noticed it walk
Taking many stiff strides across the grass
Which is a sight I've not seen before and

Its gait on its spindly legs reminded
Me of a portly formally dressed old
Gentleman with his hands in the pockets
Of his suitcoat as he stepped awkwardly

Along perhaps as he was attending
A funeral and casting gloom about.

I suppose
once in a while
a crow needs to
exercise its legs.

None of us has any excuse to be
Bored as we can always give ourselves to
The birds as a grey catbird casts a spell
On me on a video as the bird

Mimics a green-winged teal a Wilson's snipe
A Western kingbird a Western bluebird
A Western meadowhawk a rock hen a
Spotted towhee a red-wing blackbird and

A Pacific tree frog and I didn't
Glean the knowledge of these birds myself through
Years of observation because I could
Rely on the expert from the Cornell

Lab but now it's incumbent on me to
Open my ears and eyes to the marvels.

Perhaps the male grey
catbird is impressing the
female with its fine
repertoire exclaiming — "I
am a bird that gets around."

I like the Buddhist symbology of
The bodhisattva who's enlightened but
Chooses to linger within the world of
Suffering and its gender is pictured

As male or female at different times
And the transcendent being is believed
To be busy with a thousand arms and
Hands interacting and easing the plight

Of those who are burdened regardless of
Whether the hardships are obvious or
Subtle to those who suffer with sorrow
Without knowing the reasons why and who

Feel abandoned because to me it means
There's much more going on than I can know.

Unexplainable
reassurance sometimes comes
when surrendering
the burdensome perspectives
of the past and the future.

My ex-wife comes to my house to get the
Mail that continues to be misaddressed
And she always wants to greet my cat whom
She loves as they had a close connection

And I would often see them in bed with
Him lying on top of her as if he
Owned her but she has been out of the house
For a year and a half and every time

She returns Kitcat is standoffish and
I wonder whether he has forgotten
Her or he's upset that she's abandoned
Him according to his way of thinking

And yesterday after she left again
I saw Kitcat motionless on a chair.

Kitcat can't express
emotions with words and I
don't suppose he
distinguishes feelings but
I suspect that he was sad.

I remember how my mentor used to
Compliment the people he liked with a
Characteristically back-handed phrase
That sounded so odd to me because Cid

A master of poetry was so much
Older coming from a generation
Which invented idioms that have since
Gone out of fashion and are forgotten

And now Cid has passed decades ago and
Lives only as a memory but the
Other day in a dream the phrase he used
Anointing someone as a rebel and

A friend and a fellow traveler came
To me — he was an "offbeat" character.

In the poetry
community Cid is thought
to be among the
beatnik poets which is an
appellation he denied.

R.I.P. Cid Corman

In the process of assembling words
I don't know what I'm doing right away
As I'm starting with the impetus of a
Phrase or of an image that piques my

Curiosity and I know there is
Something within the shallows of my mind
And that I have to linger patiently
On the edge of the inexpressible

As if I were fishing in a Jon boat
And then suddenly while placing one word
Beside another I get a piercing
Insight into what it is I'm trying

To say and the whole point of a poem
Plops into a moment of clarity.

The plop creates
ripples of connections
I could have found
in no other way.

As a novice to the poetry scene
I went to readings to get my bearings
And Mike was a funny and a gritty
And sometimes a bellowing poet worn

With effort and well appreciated
In St. Paul and Minneapolis as
A guy who's been around for decades
Which I didn't know but I did sense that

He was someone who knew his way about
And with some embarrassment I showed him
The seven books that I had self-published
And he expressed mild admiration

On a gloomy winter night and he said
Often poets can't give their stuff away.

Mike Finley dubbed
the king of St. Paul poets
was busy dying
of cancer coming to terms
with an indifferent world.

Viktor Frankl was busy digging a
Ditch in the frozen ground under a gray
Sky on a gray morning dressed in his gray
Concentration camp pajamas yearning

For his wife not knowing where she was
But remembering her nurturing and
Loving encouragement when he was freed
By a perception into the secret

Of the meaning of poetry that the
"Salvation of man is through love in love"
Understanding when one has nothing left
He may yet know bliss if only in a

Moment through the loving contemplation
Within the image of his beloved.

A bird perched
on the pile of dirt
he accumulated
and peered intently
at him.

I do find myself imagining how
I am appearing to the one I love
And I'm guessing what she's thinking somehow
Contemplating the traits that I'm proud of
Replaying words we've spoken together
Taking encouragement in things she's said
Assessing the words that really matter
I could have said something better instead
I've turned her into a mirror of me
And I'm imagining what she's feeling
But I don't know if our passions agree
My distorted image is confusing
I'm lost in a hall of funhouse mirrors
The more I think — they're not getting clearer.

I just know that
I'm trying too hard to make
things happen that are
beyond my control and that
I really have to relax.

I called several times with no response
And sent several text messages too
I'm adopting a pose of nonchalance
While stymied and wondering what to do
I suppose it's my responsibility
To make the first moves and see what happens
While working on my insecurity
I may have to surrender my passion
Girls are like buses — another's coming
It's not a benefit to care so much
Our predawn calls were encouraging
But now once again we are out of touch
I have got to accept the way things are
This crazy situation is bizarre.

With a head-turning
woman like her I'd always
be wondering who
else she is talking to
and I will not live like that.

I am on a quest to discover love
I'm feeling pressure to make things happen
What she's doing I have no control of
While I get these bursts of adrenaline
I am on edge and it's sharp and jagged
And I don't know why she's being aloof
I don't like being purposely ignored
I'm not surprised that I'm not shatterproof
As I search my thoughts for explanations
I struggle with my curiosity
Suffering now for my expectations
I'd like a little reciprocity
I'm a victim of my aspirations
Solitude feels like asphyxiation.

Yeah I know that I'm
putting myself under a
massive amount of
pressure but why the hell is
she choosing not to reply?

Hello my ridiculous gyrations
You're putting me through the wringer today
With unobtainable aspirations
I'll figure this out on another day
I'm better than this — I know my value
I am not going to let you scramble my head
This crazy passion is just a snafu
So I'll think about something else instead
I'm not going to let you agitate me
I know how to meditate and be calm
Practicing serenity is my key
I know your essence — you are a pipe bomb
I'm disbelieving you my demon doubt
On another day I'll figure this out.

The lotus posture
is my dissolving machine
moving energy
along my spine through my limbs
dissipating crazy thoughts.

I know she is a social butterfly
She has plenty of opportunity
I don't know what her absence signifies
I'm not enjoying my passivity
I am going to return to match.com
Female company is available
Loneliness is a fragmentation bomb
Doing nothing isn't acceptable
I've done it before — I know what to do
I'll leave a hundred messages today
There are all these profiles to go through
And I'm certain to get some interplay
Most won't respond — but I really don't care
Nothing is happening if I don't dare.

I'm able to be
indifferent about the
massive numbers of
women online until I
get a glimpse of who they are.

During college I read a short story
About a guy with a beautiful wife
The emotion of the tale was heavy
Showing the cataclysm of his life
His wife began to drift away from him
With a separation of affection
For no reason weightier than a whim
She never gave him an explanation
She just stopped talking and left him alone
When confronted all she did was to weep
At the end of the tale his wife was gone
He had a terrible time trying to sleep
It is odd that she was the one weeping
And yet it was he who wasn't sleeping.

Who knows what really
happened between the couple
and it's possible
important facts were left out
but I feel sorry for him.

I do love listening to Alan Watts
He's a master of ancient Eastern wisdom
He's helping me with my consciousness knots
Feeding my craving for mysticism
The point of his talk is liberation
I listen to him while driving my car
His words propose a cosmic flirtation
On occasion he will reference a star
He says the star and I are related
Our existence depends on each other
Though the connections are complicated
It's true that we are woven together
I am waiting for that bolt of lightning
A change of view that is enlightening.

Alan says the more
I seek for liberation
the further away
I thrust it from me because
it cannot be seized by force.

Alan's temperament is humorous
He jokes about a goose in a bottle
There is a point — he's not gratuitous
The plight of the goose is a boondoggle
So how can we get the goose out alive?
The Zen master is stubbornly silent
There's no solution that we can contrive
It doesn't help to become more strident
The master takes another direction
It seems he's forgotten about the goose
He's even joyful in misdirection
And then he exclaims that the goose got loose
It just happened without explanation
Maybe because of its relaxation?

Alan's tale about
the Zen master and the goose
is reassuring
about liberation and
a lover's befuddlement.

Alan talks about Hindu mythmaking
He dwells upon the game of hide and seek
The Gods are laughing — the Gods are dancing
They hide their faces and then — take a peek
But how does this comport with suffering?
When we squirm and strain to escape our pain?
When the impact of life is confusing?
It's hard to determine what's most humane
Alan talks about the game of our dreams
Soon enough we'd be bored with paradise
Constant happiness is not what it seems
Perhaps our troubles are a kind of spice
We couldn't know happiness without strife
Having hardships gives meaning to a life.

The intensity
the suffering may be too
much to be borne and
yet the game continues on
perhaps to awakening.

The unhindered mind is spontaneous
With thought following thought following thought
And often they are miscellaneous
But my dilemmas come in getting caught
Liberation need not be difficult
As long as I'm not picking and choosing
When I'm yearning for a certain result
And that is when I will be suffering
Then how does one love and also succeed
With desire approaching possession?
Because I'd like to be spreading my seeds
And I'm cultivating a fixation
This girl is dangling just beyond my reach
And I'm so focused on winning my peach.

I am lingering
on the point of frustration
while practicing the
spiritual jujitsu of
a tricky relaxation.

I love the sound that a temple bell makes
It strikes the air with reverberations
It is an invitation to awake
It serves to quiet anticipations
The bell has a tone of solemnity
Which for me is also deeply joyful
It has an odd familiarity
Even though I am anxious and doubtful
It says loving peace is available
And I don't have to get what I'm seeking
When something better is obtainable
It points to an overall releasing
There's a hint that I've known such peace before
I already have what I'm looking for.

The temple bell speaks
of an underlying and
invigorating
simplicity of joyful
being just beyond yearning.

I'm living beyond the temple's borders
And all caught up with winning and losing
I'm worried about what's around the corner
And hungering for objects of my choosing
I'm dangling by a string of my desires
And the wind is making a toy of me
I'm swaying back and forth over a fire
And feeling how my thoughts are scorching me
All I have to do is simply relax
And release what I think that I must get
It is such an insanely simple act
Part of me doesn't want to do it yet
I am a fool living a comedy
Playing a part in greater harmony.

Laughing at myself
I guess is part of the game
rules as long as I'm
not taking my dilemmas
so very seriously.

Messages of peace are all around me
I love listening to wind in the leaves
It is a gentle sound of harmony
I am hearing it tumble sigh and heave
It is a sermon given wordlessly
It's really OK if I have to grieve
And to feel my emotions heartily
As they are signals for me to receive
The *dharma* functions mysteriously
I feel it when I'm listening to trees
Releasing is a possibility
I can free myself and live at my ease
All this striving is an absurdity
It is not helping and can only tease.

Relaxing is the
hardest trick for me pull
off and I do it
when I'm not even thinking
about the need to relax.

I get a sense that I shouldn't hold on
And that I shouldn't be yearning for her
There's a possibility that she's gone
And I can't get back to the way things were
Any master I've heard of can let go
They don't fight against their circumstances
They imitate the water and they flow
I am trying to accept her absence
Sometimes I wonder what she's doing now
And I have to let my mind think like this
I know these thoughts will dissipate somehow
As I am remembering our last kiss
It's funny how my thoughts are like the wind
And when I fight I summon a whirlwind.

My mind and my heart
will whirl as they do until
exhaustion taking
however long it takes and
I have to let it happen.

Once again you snare me with a surprise
I didn't expect you to call again
I forgot you know how to dramatize
I am reluctant but I can't refrain
Only you would ring me at 5 a.m.
No one else would think of calling me then
I'd say I'm not happy — but yes I am
I'd thought we'd connect but didn't know when
You give me an excuse that I can't believe
You say you're paralyzed by the divorce
And you say that I can give you relief
Because you're taking on your ex's force
Your ex-husband is being malicious
And our conversations are delicious.

I'm getting a hint
that this girl has me wrapped
around her pinky
finger and I'm a fool who
couldn't be happier.

The sky is open to the birds and I
Will see a bird or a pair of birds or a
Flock of birds flying in the sky but what
I don't see is where the birds come from

Or where they go and it's easy to
Fix my attention on the feathery
Creatures and neglect the phenomenon
Of the being of the sky that because the

Sky is what it is it has created
The birds to be what the birds have become
Fashioned into many different forms
Of various colors and habits and

I am getting only a glimpse of what
Is happening inside this special moment.

I don't know where the
birds and the sky came from and
don't know where they are
going beyond knowing that
they are woven together.

It's a paradox that when I sense that
I'm much too tense because something within
My expectations led me into a
Cul-de-sac resulting in frustration

And I have reached a point of frustration
That even though I know that I should it
Has become quite difficult to relax
So that even though I want to relax

I do have such a hard time relaxing
And yet when I don't have expectations
And I'm not thinking about the need to
Relax that is precisely when I am

Relaxed and I didn't have to earn my
Relaxation as it's something that happens.

I suppose I could
earn my relaxation by
not having any
expectations but then it's
really hard to do business.

I see a flock of starlings in a bush
And they are making a racket of chirps
And when I approach they become silent
And when I walk away they resume their

Chirping which intrigues me so that again
I approach and again they get quiet
So now I linger to see what they will
Do and after a while now and then and

One at a time they chirp at me with a
Tone I imagine of irritation
And a desire I guess that I would
Go away and leave them to their vital

Communication which to me sounds like
Obsessive and nonsensical gossip.

Perhaps the flock is
the reincarnated soul
of a gossip who
just can't stop talking and so
is now suitably punished.

At the farthest end of my bicycle
Circuit when I am climbing the final
Slope to the utmost elevation of my
Ride I have come to be on the lookout

For a certain red-wing blackbird whom I
Often see perching on one of many
Baby cottonwoods by the side of the
Road and I look forward to seeing the

Bird and hearing it chirp and fly away
As it habitually does but now
I notice sadly all the cottonwoods
After having reached a height of two feet

Have been cut down by the county mower
And going by I don't see the blackbird.

After turning for
the return trip passing
again the missing
cottonwoods I hear and see
the blackbird perched on a post.

On a Saturday afternoon at a
Gathering of my friends at a cabin
On Big Marine Lake we sit watching
A family of loons who are raising

A ruckus and aggressively paddling
Towards a kayaker who got too close
To them and so the kayaker turns and
Is leaving and yet the loons keep chasing

And we watch the drama unfold and a
Couple remarks that the loons also get
Quite agitated in the presence of
Eagles and I do not suppose that the

Eagles are quite as accommodating
As this conscientious kayaker is.

Boundaries are crossed
all the time and decisions
are made about how
aggressively to respond
depending so much on pluck.

Summer is the occasion when I can
Indulge in pleasures otherwise out of
Reach and I look forward to going to
Aldi's once a week and choosing a cart

That perhaps may have a gimpy wheel and
I speed to the bin I'm interested
In not far from the chocolate I can get
In any season so that I can gaze

At the objects of my desire in a
Large bin in the produce department and
I rap them with my knuckles and I've been
Told that it helps in choosing to look for

Yellow patches as an indicator
Of sweetness for the best watermelons.

It's a pivotal
moment when cutting into
the watermelon
and taking the first bite to
appreciate its richness.

If I were a thing of inoffensive
Temperament and not equipped with the
Teeth and prongs of predatory intent
And if all I wanted to do was to

Eat my leaves in peace as the leaves are there
In plentitude to be nibbled wouldn't
It be propitious to blend into
The anonymity and complexity

Of the woody background and I would adopt
A hesitating and a stealthy gait
And on occasion even imitate
The motion of a twig blowing in a

Breeze to avoid the imminent danger
Of exposure seizure and grisly death.

Looking like a twig
amid a billion other
woody doodads the
walking stick merges into
apprehensive quietude.

I fall into a rhythm of the mind
If I wake simmering with energy
At 3 a.m. and too alert to sleep
And the rhythm may be epitomized

As the weight of the past and the future
Which is nothing more than a phantom of
Unpleasant possibilities looming
In the darkness forming into a run

Of what-about-isms which is a way
Of peeking around the corners of what
I think happened or of what might happen
Even though in either case I know that

There's nothing to do at the moment and
It would be better if I could relax.

The propensity
of this rhythm of thought is
dissipation but
its energy dissolves and
I'm OK in the morning.

Rhythms of mind can be likened to a
Hound dog who has a funny habit of
Circling about several times before
It settles down to sleep and just when it's

On the ground and has the appearance of
Being down for the evening it will rise
And resume its circling again and it
Settles and rises and circles again

Over and over and it does no good
For an exasperated observer
To exert force or to distract the dog
With tricks as it's clear that the only thing

To do is let exhaustion do the job
To be followed by rejuvenation.

I guess you could say
that I'm trudging on the road
to liberation
and exhausting myself with
bouts of exaggeration.

The blazing
sun beats on
my leaning
torso — I
pedal my
bike like a
animal.

—*Tekkan*

www.ingramcontent.com/pod-product-compliance
Lightning Source LLC
Chambersburg PA
CBHW040107120526
44589CB00039B/2785